Sir Cumference

and the

First Round Table

A Math Adventure

Cindy Neuschwander

Illustrated by Wayne Geehan

ini Charlesbridge

For my parents, Max and Carol. – C.N.

Published by Charlesbridge
85 Main Street, Watertown, MA 02472
(617) 926-0329
www.charlesbridge.com

Printed by Sung In Printing
in Gunpo-Si, Kyonggi-Do, Korea
(hc) 15
(sc) 30

Library of Congress Cataloging-in-Publication Data
Neuschwander, Cindy.
    Sir Cumference and the first round table : a math adventure /
by Cindy Neuschwander ; illustrated by Wayne Geehan.
        p.   cm.
    Summary : Assisted by his knight, Sir Cumference, and using
ideas offered by the knight's wife and son, King Arthur finds the
perfect shape for his table.
    ISBN 978-1-57091-160-6 (reinforced for library use)
    ISBN 978-1-57091-152-1 (softcover)
    ISBN 978-1-60734-149-9 (ebook pdf)
    1. Geometry—Juvenile literature. [1. Geometry. 2. Shape.]
I. Geehan, Wayne, ill. II. Title.
QA445.5.N48 1997
516—dc21   97-5820

Long ago, in a land known as Camelot, there lived many knights and ladies. Their ruler was a mighty, but gracious, man named King Arthur. During many years of peace and good harvests, the people lived happily.

The trouble began when they saw the army of their neighbors to the north gathering at the border. These people, known as the Circumscribers, looked as if they might be preparing to make war. King Arthur called upon his bravest and most trusted knights to plan what to do.

4

The knights rode as fast as they could to the King's castle. Sir Cumference lived nearby, so his family came with him. Sir Cumference was married to Lady Di, who came from the town of Ameter.

They had a son named Radius. Radius was very small and quite young, but his keen mind and boundless energy more than made up for what he lacked in height and age.

After the first day of meetings with all the King's knights, Sir Cumference sat with Lady Di.

"Oooh," he groaned, "my throat hurts. I have to shout to be heard at the other end of that long rectangular table. Everyone has to shout, and the King is very upset."

"Why don't you fix the table?" suggested Lady Di.

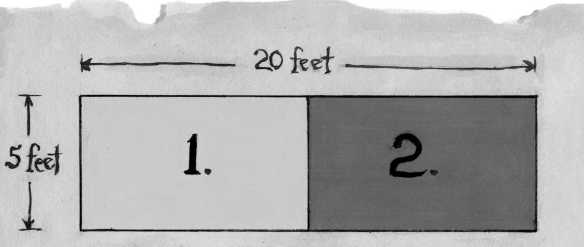

"How can we do that?" Sir Cumference asked.

"Well," said Lady Di, "you could cut it in half.
Look, here is a drawing of the table.
It has two long sides and two short sides.
If you cut it in half, and put the two halves side-by-side,
you will have a table with four equal sides."

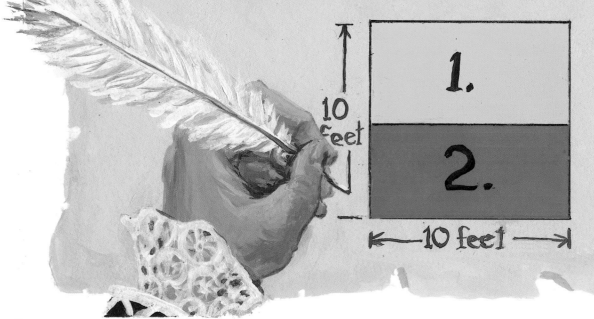

"Lady Di, what a good idea!" Sir Cumference called for the carpenter, Geo of Metry. Geo began work immediately.

The next day the new table was ready. Everyone commented on the wonderful, square shape. However, another problem arose.

At each corner of the table, the knights whispered to each other while someone else was talking.

Sir Galahad exclaimed, "King Arthur, how can we meet to discuss a solution when people talk secretly to each other?"

"Sir Galahad is correct," King Arthur responded. "We have come here to talk of defending our land against the Circumscribers, not to talk in secrecy."

After the meeting, King Arthur told Sir Cumference a new table was needed. That night, Sir Cumference told Lady Di about the problems with the square table.

Lady Di thought a moment and then said, "What if we cut the square table diagonally? We could put the two halves together to make a diamond."

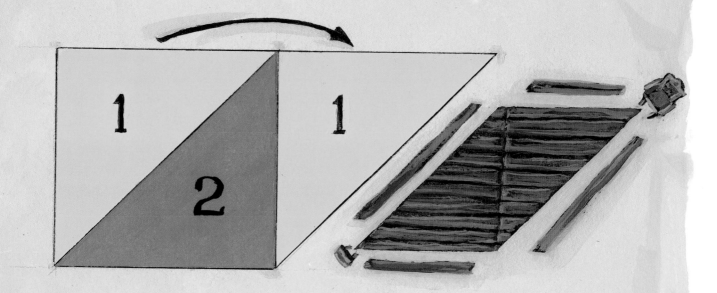

She drew a diagram and said, "The King could sit at one end, and you could sit at the opposite end. Everyone would be close enough to hear, but the knights would not be in any tight corners."

After seeing the plan, Sir Cumference agreed that it was a good idea. Geo, the carpenter, said, "In carpentry class they called this shape a parallelogram. I will have the table ready by the morrow."

The next day, Sir Lancelot and Sir Gawain were amazed to see a table in the shape of a parallelogram. The others liked it, but King Arthur was not happy sitting at the sharp point.

The King let the knights have jousting practice and swordplay while he spoke with Sir Cumference.

"Sir Cumference, the point of the table sticks into me like a sword! We need to think about ways to prevent war, but this table makes me feel like fighting! Can you fix it?"

"I will do my best, Sire," said Sir Cumference.

That afternoon he stood by the field and watched the others joust. It was a beautiful day, with blue skies, and flags flapping in the breeze. Sir Gawain's flag was blue with a white cross, Sir Lancelot's flag was green with lions, and Sir Torre's flag was green with an eagle. The flags were all similar in shape: they were all triangles.

"That's it," said Sir Cumference, "a triangular table!"

Sir Cumference called Geo and explained. Geo said, "If we cut the parallelogram table in half, that would leave two triangles. One triangle might be too small."

So they measured the proposed triangular table, and realized that four people could not fit on each side. "Geo, let's think some more," said Sir Cumference, and he went to discuss shapes with Lady Di.

"**Y**es," said Lady Di. "The triangles would be too small, so cut off the corners like this and make an octagon. Look, it will solve the problem."

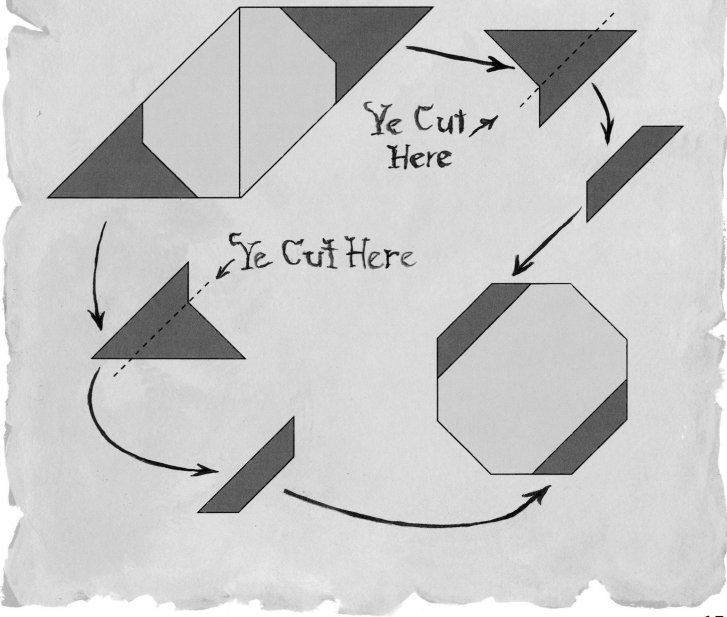

When the knights sat at the octagon table, each one wanted a side all to himself. Eight sides and twelve knights! Who would share a side with another?

They agreed that the King should have a side all to himself, because he was their leader, but that left seven sides and twelve people.

"Knights, let there be order," said King Arthur calmly.

"We need to remember that we are here for the defense of our land. How can we talk at this table with its problem of corners and sides? Sir Cumference, have the carpenter build a table shaped like an egg, and perhaps then we will behave more like a flock."

Sir Cumference drew up plans for an oval table for Geo.

"This table is going to be harder to build since it has no straight edges," said Geo. "I will begin at once."

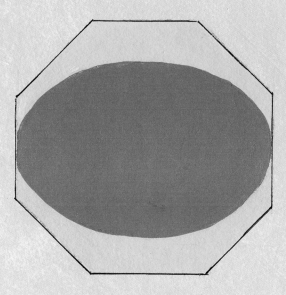

When the knights met again they were all impressed by the oval table. Sir Lancelot suggested that they raise their goblets and drink a toast.

All of the knights raised their goblets, but there was a great commotion from the ends of the table.

The knights at the end of the oval table bumped into the King as they raised their goblets. No one had enough room.

Some of the knights began to argue. Then King Arthur shouted, "STOP! All leave me until tomorrow, except for Sir Cumference."

After talking to King Arthur, Sir Cumference returned home discouraged once again.

Radius piped up, "Father, when I have a problem I cannot solve, I do something else for a while. Why don't we go for a ride?"

That afternoon, Sir Cumference, Radius, and Lady Di went riding. No one said much until Radius shouted, "Father, look! A tree has fallen over!"

"So it has," observed the knight.

"**D**on't you see, Father? There's your table!"

Lady Di got off her horse for a closer look. She stood on her tiptoes and stretched her arm up as high as it could go. Her fingertips just met the upper edge of the trunk.

"It should be big enough," she said. "This part is as tall as I can reach, and the wood seems to be of good quality."

Sir Cumference summoned Geo to cut a cross-section of the trunk to make into a tabletop.

"Leave the bark on the outside edge," he told Geo, "I like its rough feel."

Geo and his helpers sawed through the huge tree trunk. Then they hoisted the heavy slab into an oxcart, and off they went to Geo's workshop. Geo worked all night building the new table.

When the knights met the next day, the table was finished. Everyone was content. No one shouted or whispered. No one felt cornered or trapped. No one was poked in the stomach, and no one felt squished.

Everyone had an equal position around the table. As they talked, they decided the best plan was to try to make peace with their neighbors. King Arthur was so pleased that he announced they would celebrate that night.

Soon, everyone was enjoying the music, dancing, and banquet. Suddenly, the music stopped. A messenger rushed in and handed a sealed parchment to King Arthur. The King read it and smiled.

"Ladies, knights, and guests, I have excellent news. The Circumscribers are not planning an attack. They want only to measure the area of their kingdom. There will be peace in the land!"

"**H**ooray!" Everyone cheered 'til the King held up his hand for silence.

"To honor these knights who gathered at this table to save our kingdom, let them henceforth be known as the Knights of the Round Table.

"Let us thank Sir Cumference and Lady Di, and their son Radius. They made this round table possible." Everyone cheered again.

"**F**urthermore, because Lady Di of Ameter has a reach that is equal to the distance across the table, we will name this measurement for her. We will call it the diameter."

"I am proud of Radius, too," added King Arthur. "Someday he will become a fine knight. He may be small but he has tall ideas." Everyone nodded and clapped. "Let us call this small measurement from the center of the circle to its edge the radius."

RADIUS

"**F**inally, let us not forget our clever Sir Cumference. Since it was his idea to leave the bark on the outside edge of our table, we will name the outside edge of any circle after him. Let us call it the circumference."

CIRCUMFERENCE

Sir Cumference bowed to the King as everyone rose
from their seats and began cheering and whistling and
stomping their feet. It was the happiest celebration that
anyone could remember.